Amelia Boman

COPYRIGHT NOTICE
All rights reserved. No part of this publication may be reproduced, distributed, or transmitted in any form or by any means, including photocopying, recording, or other electronic or mechanical methods, without the prior written permission of the author, except in the case of brief quotations embodied in critical reviews.

CPSIA information can be obtained
at www.ICGtesting.com
Printed in the USA
LVHW070300301120
672999LV00033B/495